Meet me on™
JEKYLL ISLAND

Meet me on™
JEKYLL ISLAND

TIMELESS IMAGES AND FLAVORFUL RECIPES
FROM GEORGIA'S REMARKABLE ISLAND RETREAT

Mary Lawson
Editor

Daisy King
Recipe Editor

Historic Hospitality Books

Historic Hospitality Books

Meet me on Jekyll Island was published by Historic Hospitality Books in collaboration with *The Jekyll Island Authority* and *Jekyll Island Club Hotel*. Historic Hospitality Books creates exquisitely designed custom books for America's iconic hotels, inns, resorts, spas, and historic destinations. Historic Hospitality Books is an imprint of Southwestern Publishing Group, Inc., 2451 Atrium Way, Nashville, Tennessee, 37214. Southwestern Publishing Group is a wholly owned subsidiary of Southwestern/Great American, Inc., Nashville, Tennessee.

Christopher G. Capen, President, Southwestern Publishing Group
Sheila Thomas, President and Publisher, Historic Hospitality Books

Editor: Mary Lawson
Recipe Editor: Daisy King
Cover Designer: LeAnna Massingille

Special thanks to John Hunter, Kevin Runner, Patty Henning, and Harlan Hambright for their assistance in the development of this book.

ISBN: 978-0-87197-562-1
Library of Congress Control Number: 2016943021

Printed in China

10 9 8 7 6 5 4

JEKYLL ISLAND

Jekyll Island, often referred to as "Georgia's Jewel," is one of her most beautiful coastal barrier islands. Rich with history as an exclusive retreat for some of our nation's most wealthy, the Jekyll Island Club still remains her crowning glory.

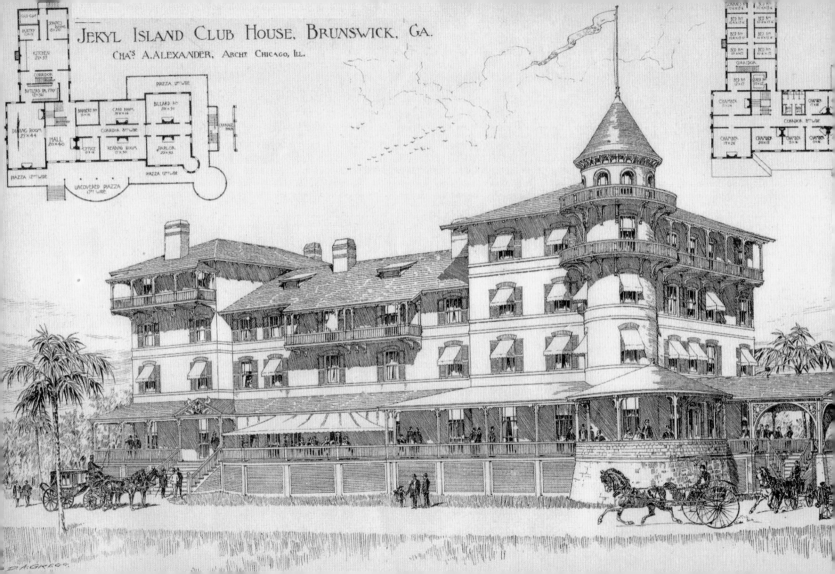

JEKYL ISLAND CLUB HOUSE, BRUNSWICK, GA.

CHAS A. ALEXANDER, ARCHT CHICAGO, ILL.

HISTORY IN THE MAKING

Native Americans, Spanish missionaries, English colonists, enslaved Africans, and French planters were all a part of the early history of Jekyll Island. It was, however, General James Oglethorpe who founded the colony of Georgia in 1733 and gave the island its present name. He sent Major William Horton to Jekyll to set up an outpost to help protect Fort Frederica on St. Simons Island, and Major Horton built it into a relatively prosperous plantation prior to his death in 1749. Christophe Poulain DuBignon, who immigrated from France to escape the French Revolution, purchased Jekyll in 1792. The DuBignons cultivated Sea Island cotton using slave labor and developed a successful business on their plantation until the Civil War. After the war, most of the island was sold in parcels and divided among several family members, and John Eugene DuBignon, the great-grandson of Christophe, purchased the southern portion of the island from his relatives. DuBignon and his brother-in-law, Newton Finney, decided to take advantage of the southern resort boom of the 1880s and conceived the idea to sell the entire island to a club composed of wealthy men as a perfect site for a hunting club. In 1886, the lofty plan succeeded and DuBignon sold the island to the newly formed Jekyll Island Club, which was to become the most exclusive social club in the United States.

A PLAN FOR THE WEALTHY

The Jekyll Island Club would be a place for tycoons, politicians, and social-ites to revel in their own luxury and America's burgeoning wealth. Club officers hired Chicago architect Charles A. Alexander to design an elegant, yet simple, clubhouse which took advantage of the natural setting the island provided. When the clubhouse opened in 1887, it had indoor plumbing and was illuminated by gas fixtures. The building itself is an example of Queen Anne architecture with its asymmetrical plan, wrap around porches, towers, and decorative features such as spindles and lattice. Telephone service was added in 1898, electricity in 1903, and an elevator in 1916. At a time when the idea of a modern seaside resort was still a novelty, members experienced levels of luxury and service that were remarkable. Members and their guests enjoyed morning hunting, horseback riding, skeet shooting, golf, lawn bowling (known as boce), tennis, biking, picnics and lawn parties, leisurely afternoons on the beach, and carriage rides. Dinner each evening, however, was the high point of the day as the dining room grew rich with white-clad waiters, bow-tied gentlemen and stately women. Renowned chefs from New York's best restaurants staffed the kitchen. Menus featured fine wines and fresh game caught on the island. It is said that when the Jekyll Island Club members dined together, one sixth of the world's wealth (at that time) was gathered in one room!

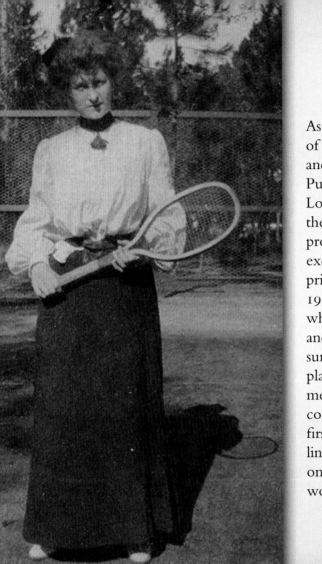

PLAY AND POWER

As an exclusive retreat for the nation's wealthiest financiers and industrialists of the time, members prized the island for its "sense of splendid isolation," and well they should. They included such notables as J. P. Morgan, Joseph Pulitzer, William K. Vanderbilt, William Rockefeller, Vincent Astor, Pierre Lorillard, and Marshall Field, to name a few. Other recognizable names on the roster were Macy, Goodyear, and Gould. Interestingly, the club proclaimed from the beginning that it was not intended to be "a selfish and exclusive man's club" but that "ladies . . . will be freely admitted to all the privileges." The first woman did indeed join in 1893, and by the end of the 1930s, approximately 25 percent of the club members were female, many of whom enjoyed hunting the island's abundant supply of deer, quail, pheasant, and other game that had been imported to the island. The mystique surrounding this resort is not limited to its reputation for being an opulent playground for the nation's elite, however. It was also the site of events and meetings of historic significance during the turn of the century. Due to the concentration of internationally prominent business leaders on the island, the first transcontinental telephone call took place there in 1915 and included a link to AT&T president Vail, in the clubhouse. In addition, the meeting rooms on the first floor were suited for the group that convened to draft the framework for the Aldrich Act in 1910, which became the Federal Reserve Act.

MILLIONAIRE ACCOMMODATIONS

The Jekyll Island wharf was the gateway and initial gathering point for the club members upon arrival to their winter retreat. Members and their guests either traveled to Brunswick by train and then came over to Jekyll via boats, or they journeyed by yacht. Upon their arrival, carriages waited to take them to the clubhouse to register and then be escorted to their accommodations. The initial members of the new hunting club on the island playground had each purchased shares for six hundred dollars apiece which included a plot of land on the island. When the clubhouse became too crowded for the elite guests, they began to build their own mansion-sized "cottages" designed to house entire families with staff. Though the cottages were simple in comparison to their lavish homes in the north, they certainly met the comfort levels to which they were accustomed. In addition to the cottages, a six-unit building, considered to be one of the first condominiums constructed in this country, was built in 1896 by a five-man syndicate composed of William Rockefeller, Henry B. Hyde, James A. Scrymser, Joseph Stickney, and William P. Anderson, who financed the construction of the Sans Souci Apartments (French for "without care.") Finally in 1901 an annex of eight privately owned apartments was attached to the clubhouse.

DISILLUSIONED AND DISBURSED

The Jekyll Island Club flourished into the 1930s, but world events took their toll. Memberships began to decline dramatically. The Jekyll Island Club members became disenchanted with the island and began traveling to European spas and elsewhere for their entertainment. They were less eager to provide financial support for the club, and at the end of the 1932 season there was a deficit of $28,000. The recruiting of new "associate" memberships for drastically reduced fees kept the club afloat for a time, but the Depression took its toll. With the advent of World War I, several members offered their personal yachts to the war effort as well as financial assistance. The final blow to the life of the club, however, was World War II and the shortage of labor and rationing that resulted. Members left the island in 1942, and the era of the Jekyll Island Club was over. The club's president had hoped to reopen it after the war, but it never happened. The club's members never went back. World War II brought an end to the club era and in its wake, epochal changes in tourism in general.

A PUBLIC CHANGE

A larger middle class population in the post-war years created a need for affordable tourist accommodations. In 1947 the state of Georgia condemned the island and paid the remaining members $675,000 in order to turn the once prestigious and influential island retreat into a public state park. Jekyll's period of isolation as a millionaires' retreat had ended, and its era as a state park with accessibility for the common man began. The predominant use of the automobile had made the coastal areas accessible to a greater number of people. In order to lure the tourists who traveled by car through Georgia en route to Florida, there was a need for automobile accessibility to the island. A multimillion-dollar project to build a state-financed causeway and bridge to Jekyll was unveiled, but it would be another seven years before the island was finally accessible by automobile. The state attempted, until 1972, to operate the clubhouse, Sans Souci, and Crane Cottage as a hotel complex, but its efforts were unsuccessful and the buildings were closed. In 1978, the 240-acre club district was designated a National Historic Landmark. In 1985, work began to restore the clubhouse, annex, and the Sans Souci into a world-class hotel and resort. The $20 million in restoration funds have all been invested in the buildings and grounds.

SOMETHING FOR EVERYONE

Today, the Jekyll Island Club National Historic Landmark District is an enchanting riverfront compound and one of the largest, ongoing restoration projects in the southeastern United States. Most of the Club's historic structures have been restored, and the club itself is once again a showcase. Today, maintenance in the historic district is continual and thirty-three buildings from the late nineteenth and early twentieth centuries including mansion-sized cottages, some of which exist as museums, art galleries, or bookstores surround the island's centerpiece, the enormous Jekyll Island Club Hotel. Guided tours through the landmark are offered as well as first-class hotel accommodations in the hotel itself and an abundance of activities from relaxing on its beautiful beaches to golf, tennis, camping, picnicking, biking, fishing, and boating as well as horseback riding through maritime forests and dolphin tours in the Atlantic Ocean. The salt marshes may be explored by kayak or canoe to enjoy the island's natural beauty and indigenous wildlife. Jekyll Island also offers several significant birding sites for migrating species as well as the rare opportunity to observe nearly extinct loggerhead sea turtles and other coastal life in its natural habitat. Once a paradise island hosting the most elite, inaccessible club in the world, its moss draped oaks, golden marshes, and remote beaches now welcome everyone to enjoy the simple pleasures and elegant surroundings of this longtime beloved vacation destination and grand Georgia historic landmark.

MILLIONAIRE COTTAGES

TO EACH HIS OWN

From 1888 to 1928 club members constructed fourteen "cottages" in addition to the ones that had been built by DuBignon in 1884 in the location we now know as the Historic District. They were much in keeping with the idea of simplicity, though definitely large by ordinary standards. Queen Anne and shingle styles were predominant during the early years, while later cottages reflected architectural trends of Italian Renaissance and Spanish eclectic styles.

DuBignon Cottage

In 1884, John Eugene DuBignon built a new farmhouse early in the club era, which was called Club Cottage for the longest period of the club era and was used to house overflow guests of the club. It became known as the "Superintendent's cottage" and was the home of E. G. Grob, who served as the Jekyll Island Club's resident manager for forty-two years.

FURNESS COTTAGE/INFIRMARY

Philadelphian Walter Rogers Furness built this cottage in 1890, and in 1930 Frank Goodyear bought it and donated it to be used as the club infirmary. It was moved to its present site. From 1930 till 1942, it was a fully equipped facility staffed by doctors from Johns Hopkins Hospital during the season of January to April.

HOLLYBOURNE COTTAGE

Hollybourne was built in 1890 by Charles Stewart Maurice, an engineer and a partner in the Union Bridge Company. It is the only cottage built during the club era with island's native tabby, a building material unique to the South Carolina and Georgia coastal area.

INDIAN MOUND COTTAGE

Indian Mound was constructed in 1892 as an original shingle/stick style cottage for inventor Gordon McKay. After his death, William Rockefeller, a director of Standard Oil, purchased the cottage. It later became a twenty-five-room winter home for the Rockefeller family.

MOSS COTTAGE

William Struthers Jr., retired owner of a Philadelphia marble works, engaged in the erection of hundreds of monuments and marble buildings throughout the nineteenth century, constructed Moss Cottage (named after Spanish moss so prevalent on Jekyll Island) in 1896 using all local materials including cypress shingles. He had the distinction of being the first person to bring a motorcar onto the island, only to have it voted off because of the noise. Later Moss Cottage was the winter home of George Henry Macy, tobacconist of Hudson, New York, who became president of Union Pacific Tea (later A&P).

CHICHOTA COTTAGE

Chichota Cottage was built in 1897 for David H. King Jr. of New York, two stone lions stand guard over the ruins of Chichota Cottage. In 1900, the cottage was sold to Edwin Gould, son of railroad magnate and financier Jay Gould. The cottage was abandoned after the Gould's son died accidentally in a hunting accident, and it was torn down in 1941. The foundations and courtyard pool remain.

MISTLETOE COTTAGE

Mistletoe Cottage was designed as a Dutch Colonial Revival house in 1900 for Henry Kirk Porter, a U.S. Representative from Pennsylvania and a manufacturer of light locomotives. In 1926, John Claflin, a New York dry goods manufacturer (Lord and Taylor) purchased the cottage. He was the last living charter member of the club, and he died in 1938.

PULITZER-ALBRIGHT COTTAGE

The Pulitzer Cottage was built in 1903 by Joseph Pulitzer, editor of the St. Louis Post Dispatch and New York World, whose bequests established the School (now Graduate School) of Journalism at Columbia University and the Pulitzer Prize program. It would later become a twenty-six-room island residence. After Pulitzer's death, John Albright, art patron and coal magnate of New York, purchased the cottage.

Goodyear Cottage

The Goodyear Cottage was built from 1903 to 1906 for Frank Henry Goodyear, a lumber baron and railroad industrialist from Buffalo, New York who died in 1907 shortly after the completion of his cottage. His widow and children continued to use the cottage for some years after his death. The building now houses the Jekyll Island Arts Association.

Cherokee Cottage

The Cherokee Cottage was constructed in 1904 as an Italian Renaissance style cottage reflecting the tastes of Dr. and Mrs. G. F. Shrady of New York for whom it was originally built by their son-in-law, Edwin Gould. It was Gould's desire to have the Shrady cottage nearby so that he and his wife could enjoy her parents' company. The Gould's owned more buildings in the club compound than any other family.

Courtesy of the Jekyll Island Museum Archives

CRANE COTTAGE

Crane Cottage was built in 1917 on the site of an earlier cottage, Solterra, which was built in 1890 for Frederick Baker and destroyed by fire in 1914. Richard Teller Crane Jr., of Chicago purchased the site and built the largest private residence constructed by a club member. As an Italian villa, the Crane Cottage was the most expensive and elegant winter home ever built at Jekyll, and its design and construction represented a distinct shift in club appearance from rustic to more lavish accommodations, boasting seventeen bathrooms and a formal sunken garden with fountains and upper terrace. It incorporated an enclosed courtyard, formal garden, and a reflecting pool.

VILLA OSPO

The Villa Ospo was built from 1927 to 1928, it was designed by architect John Russell Pope, who also designed the National Gallery of Art in Washington, D.C. for Walter Jennings, a director in the Standard Oil Company. It is the only cottage in the district to have been built with a garage.

32

Villa Marianna

The Villa Marianna was completed in 1928, as the last cottage to be built during the club era, it is a beautiful representation of Spanish architecture. Frank Miller Gould (second son of Edwin Gould) included such features as a wonderful square tower that provided a special view of the club compound and the marsh. The breezeway observatory overlooking the walled courtyard, Italian style fireplace, and reflecting pool make it a favorite for wedding receptions.

WHITE BEAN AND COLLARD GREEN SOUP

1	pound dried white beans, soaked 1 day	3	tablespoons minced garlic
1	pound cooked collard greens, about 4 pounds raw	2	links (about 1/2 pound) Andouille sausage, grilled and small diced
3	tablespoons salad oil	1	gallon chicken stock
1	cup chopped Vidalia onions		salt and pepper to taste

Assemble ingredients and utensils. In advance, put dried beans in a large pot and cover with water. Cover and let stand overnight or for 8 hours. Broil sausage in oven on a pan with a rack. Cool, dice, and set aside. Wash 4 pounds of fresh collard greens, remove tough stems and cut crosswise into strips about 1–1 1/2 inches thick. In a large pot, bring 8 cups of water to a boil. Add the collards in batches, let each batch wilt before adding the next one, and cook until tender, about 15 minutes. Do not overcook. Cool, strain. In a heavy bottomed stock pot, heat oil until just at the smoking point and add onions, garlic, and sausage. Sauté until onions are clear. Add stock and bring to a boil. Drain beans and add to the stock mixture. Bring back to boil and reduce heat and simmer for 1 1/2 hours or until beans are done. Add collards and adjust seasoning with salt and cracked pepper.

Yields 8 to 10 servings

SHRIMP RABBIT

2	pounds shrimp, cooked in the shell	1	teaspoon dry mustard
3	tablespoons butter		Worcestershire sauce to taste
2	cups grated Gruyere or Swiss cheese		salt and freshly ground pepper to taste
2	cups grated Cheddar cheese	1/2	cup dry white wine
1/2	cup heavy cream		toast points
2	eggs, lightly beaten		

Assemble ingredients and utensils. Peel and devein the shrimp. If small, leave whole; if large, cut into bite-sized pieces. Melt the butter in a saucepan and stir in the cheeses. Stir until the cheese is melted. Add the cream and eggs, then the remaining ingredients except toast. Stir until mixture is slightly thickened and smooth. Stir in the shrimp and heat thoroughly. Serve with toast points.

Yields 6 servings

SWEET CORN CUSTARD

2 cups fresh corn cut (about 4 ears)	1/2 teaspoon salt
3 eggs beaten	1/8 teaspoon black pepper
3/4 cup (3 ounces) shredded cheddar cheese	1/8 teaspoon ground nutmeg
1/4 cup all-purpose flour	2 cups half-and-half
4 teaspoons sugar	2 tablespoons unsalted butter, melted
	salt and pepper to taste

Assemble ingredients and utensils. Combine corn, eggs, and cheese in a large bowl, stirring well. Combine flour, sugar, salt, pepper, and nutmeg; add to corn mixture. Stir in half-and-half and butter. Pour mixture into a lightly greased 1 1/2-quart shallow baking dish. Place dish in a 13x9x2 inch pan; add hot water to baking pan to a depth of 1 inch up sides of pan. Bake, uncovered, for 1 hour in a 325-degree oven, or until a knife inserted in center comes out clean.

Yields 6 to 8 servings

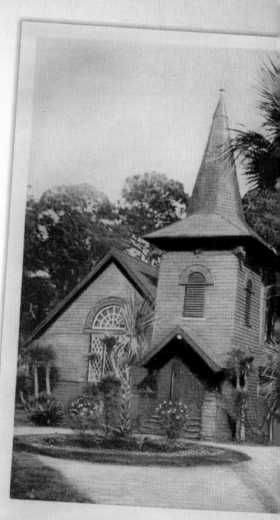

CHAPEL

PRESIDENTIAL VISIT AND SOLTERRA COTTAGE

Ironically, the cottage that had enjoyed the most historic visibility at Jekyll Island later burned to the ground, leaving its claim to fame in ashes. On March 20, 1899, President William McKinley arrived on Jekyll Island at the invitation of Cornelius Bliss, his former Secretary of the Interior and a long-standing club member. Frederic and Frances Baker, who owned Solterra Cottage, once the largest cottage on Jekyll Island, were abroad that season and graciously made their twelve-room Queen Anne shingle-style cottage available to President McKinley and his party, which also included Mrs. McKinley, Vice President Garrett A. Hobart, and his wife. It was at Solterra Cottage that the president greeted Jekyll Island Club Members who had wealth and connections to influence his presidential prospects in the 1900 elections. He departed the island on March 22, calling his stay on Jekyll Island "simply delightful." Sadly, Solterra Cottage was destroyed by fire on March 9, 1914 and only a single, small architectural remnant remains of the beautiful structure where the president once stayed. A dovecote, used to raise pigeons or doves in Solterra's backyard, survived the blaze. The last piece of a splendid structure, the dovecote has now been preserved near where Solterra once stood.

APPLE RIBBON PIE

6–8	tart apples		2	tablespoons butter or margarine
	pastry for 2-crust pie			
1	cup sugar		1/4	cup grated sharp Cheddar cheese
1	tablespoon all-purpose flour			
1/4	teaspoon nutmeg		1 1/2	teaspoons poppy seed
1/2	teaspoon cinnamon			

Assemble ingredients and utensils. Pare and core apples; slice thin. Line 9-inch pie pan with pastry. Combine sugar, flour, and spices and rub a little of mixture into pastry in pie pan. Fill pie pan with sliced apples; add remaining sugar mixture. Dot with butter or margarine. Divide remaining pastry into two equal portions. Roll out 1 portion 1/8-inch thick; top with grated cheese; fold over in 3 layers; roll out again. Cut into 5 strips 10 inches long by 3/4-inch wide. Repeat with remaining portion of pastry, using poppy seed instead of cheese. Weave strips (lattice fashion) on pie, alternating cheese strips and poppy seed strips; trim and flute edge. Bake in a 425-degree oven for 40 to 45 minutes, or until apples are tender.

Yields 6 to 8 servings

JEKYLL ISLAND CRAB CAKES

7–8	ounces lump crabmeat, (try not to break up lumps)
1	ounce mayonnaise
	juice of one lemon
1	egg, beaten

1/2	cup saltine cracker crumbs, divided and crushed by hand
	dash of sherry
	dash Old Bay seasoning
	salt and pepper to taste

Assemble ingredients and utensils. Mix mayo, sherry, lemon juice, egg, and Old Bay. Fold in crab and 1/4 cup cracker crumbs, mix gently. Adjust seasoning with salt and pepper. Using a 2-ounce scoop, scoop the mix onto a half pan that has been dusted with the cracker crumbs. Let set in cooler and then gently coat outside of the crab cakes with the crackers. Wrap tightly and chill until ready to use. Heat skillet over medium heat and add a tablespoon of olive oil or butter. Lightly coat cakes with cracker crumbs and sear over medium heat until golden brown, on the first side, then flip the cakes over and finish in a 350-degree oven for 5 minutes. Serve immediately with Lemon Peach Marmalade.

Yields 4 2-ounce cakes

LEMON PEACH MARMALADE

2	lemons, deseeded and sliced
1	pound fresh peaches, chopped
1	cup water

1 3/4	ounces pectin or clear gelatin
2 1/2	cups sugar

Assemble ingredients and utensils. In a large saucepot, add sliced lemons and cover with water. Cook for twenty minutes over low heat. Add peaches to pot and mix well. Add pectin or gelatin to pot and bring to a rolling boil, stirring constantly. Add sugar and bring again to full boil. Cook one minute, stirring constantly. Remove from heat and skim foam from the top. Cool and store in the refrigerator to set. Serve with crab cakes.

Yields 1 quart

Courtesy of the Jekyll Island Club's Chef's collection.

CRANBERRY RASPBERRY SALAD

1	3-ounce package raspberry gelatin		1	16-ounce can jellied cranberry sauce
1	3-ounce package lemon gelatin		1	7-ounce bottle lemon-lime carbonated beverage
1 1/2	cups boiling water			
1	10-ounce package frozen raspberries			

Assemble ingredients and utensils. Dissolve gelatin in boiling water. Stir in frozen berries, breaking up large pieces. Break up cranberry sauce with fork. Stir into mixture. Chill until partially set. Carefully pour in soda, stirring gently. Pour into 6-cup ring mold. Chill 5 to 6 hours overnight. Unmold onto crisp greens. May be garnished with a poached sliced apple.

Yields 8 to 10 servings

CURRIED SHRIMP SALAD

1/4	cup chopped onions	1	cup diced celery
1	tablespoon vinegar	1/4	cup diced green pepper
2	tablespoons vegetable oil	2 1/2	cups cooked shrimp
1/2	teaspoon curry powder	3/4	cup mayonnaise
1 1/2	cups cooked rice		salad greens

Assemble ingredients and utensils. Combine onion, vinegar, oil, and curry powder in a bowl. Stir in rice. Chill at least 2 hours to blend flavors. Just before serving add celery, green pepper, and shrimp. Add mayonnaise and mix lightly. Serve on salad greens.

Yields 6 servings

PRALINE CHEESECAKE

1	cup graham crackers, crushed	1 1/4	cups dark brown sugar
3	tablespoons sugar	2	tablespoons all-purpose flour
3	tablespoons butter, melted	3	eggs
3	8-ounce packages cream cheese, softened	1 1/2	teaspoons vanilla
		1	cup pecans, finely chopped
			Maple syrup

Assemble ingredients and utensils. Combine graham cracker crumbs, sugar, and butter. Press into bottom of 9-inch spring form pan. Bake at 350 degrees for 10 minutes. In large bowl of mixer, blend cream cheese, brown sugar, and flour. Add eggs, one at a time, beating well after each addition. Add vanilla and 1/2 cup pecans; mix well. Pour into crumb crust. Bake in a preheated 350-degree oven for 50 to 55 minutes. Loosen from rim and cool. Remove sides of pan. Chill. Brush with maple syrup. Sprinkle with remaining pecans.

Yields 8 to 10 servings

SWEET POTATO AND BOURBON SOUP

3 tablespoons butter	1/4 to 1/3 cup bourbon
4 medium sweet potatoes, peeled and sliced	1/2 teaspoon salt freshly ground black pepper
6 cups chicken stock	

Assemble ingredients and utensils. Heat the butter in a large skillet or heavy saucepan. Add a layer of sweet potatoes and brown on both sides. Repeat the layering and browning until all potatoes are browned. Add 5 cups of chicken stock. Cook, covered, until potatoes are tender. When tender remove potatoes and mash to a chunky texture. Blend in remaining cup of chicken stock and stir until soup becomes a medium thick consistency. Add bourbon and bring to a boil. Season with salt and pepper.

Yields 4 to 6 servings

MARINATED MUSHROOM SALAD

1/2 pound raw mushrooms	1–2 drops Tabasco
1 medium sweet onion, thinly sliced	1/2 teaspoon salt
1/2 cup olive oil	2 teaspoons minced parsley
1/4 cup tarragon wine vinegar	1 med. head iceberg lettuce

Assemble ingredients and utensils. Rinse mushrooms and pat dry. Slice lengthwise, through stems. Combine mushrooms and onions in salad bowl and pour salad oil, vinegar, Tabasco, salt, and parsley over them and mix gently. Cover bowl, let stand at room temperature for at least 4 hours. Wash lettuce, drain well. Just before serving, break lettuce into serving bowl, add tomato, mix.

Yields 4 servings

JEKYLL ISLAND MAPLE SWEET POTATO BISQUE
WITH BLUE CRAB

3	pounds sweet potatoes cut in half lengthwise	2	teaspoons black pepper	
1	Vidalia onion, peeled quartered	2	teaspoons butter	
1/4	cup olive oil	3	carrots, peeled, diced	
2	dashes nutmeg	2	stalks celery, diced	
2	dashes ground allspice	1/2	cup plus 1/2 cup sherry	
	dash cinnamon	3	quarts chicken broth	
1/4	cup, plus 3/4 cup maple syrup	3-4	cups heavy cream	
1	tablespoon kosher salt		salt and pepper to taste	
			Blue Crab meat as needed to taste	

Assemble ingredients and utensils. Mix together the nutmeg, allspice, cinnamon, 1/4 cup syrup, salt and pepper. Add the olive oil to it and mix well. Lightly rub the potatoes and onions with the oil mix and put cut side down on a roasting pan. Roast in 350-degree oven until the potatoes are tender to the touch. While waiting for the potatoes, in a large pot, sauté the carrots and celery in the butter until translucent. Add 1/2 cup sherry and reduce by half. Add the chicken stock. Pull the skins from the potatoes and scrape any drippings from the pan into the pot. Add potatoes, onions, and 3/4 cup syrup to the pot and mix well. Bring the soup to a simmer and cook for 15 min. Puree the soup and add the cream. Bring back to a simmer and then adjust seasonings with salt and pepper. Pull off the heat, add the 1/2 cup of sherry and cool it off or serve immediately.

Yields 1 gallon

Courtesy of the Jekyll Island Club's Chef's collection.

JEKYLL ISLAND TOMATOES COLLINWOOD

2	large tomatoes, star cut and halved	3	ounces bacon bits, chopped
16	ounces large curd cottage cheese	4	ounces mayonnaise
1	bunch green onions, diced (Save 4 strips for garnish.)	2	bacon strips, cooked salt, pepper, and Old Bay seasoning to taste

Assemble ingredients and utensils. Star cut and half two tomatoes, scoop out halves. Dice inside of tomatoes and save. Squeeze cottage cheese nearly dry. Put into a bowl; add onions, bacon bits, mayonnaise, and seasonings. Mix well. Scoop into tomato halves. Garnish with bacon and green onions.

Yields 4 servings

Courtesy of the Jekyll Island Club's Chef's collection.

63

OPENING OF THE FIRST TRANSCONTINENTAL LINE

A gathering spot for prominent internationally known business leaders, Jekyll Island was the perfect place in which to house the first transcontinental telephone call over public transmission lines. Theodore N. Vail, the first president of the American Telephone & Telegraph Company (AT&T), was a member of the Jekyll Island Club. The actual telephone line stretched between San Francisco and New York City. Four copper wires were held up by 130,000 wood poles. On the day of the historic phone call, approximately 1,500 AT&T employees were positioned across the entire length of the line, east to west, and on the line between Jekyll Island and New York City. The workers were prepared to fix or repair any problem that might impede the ceremonial phone call. The January 25, 1915 opening ceremony consisted of a four-way call between Jekyll Island, New York City, San Francisco, and Washington, D.C. where President Woodrow Wilson listened in from the Oval Office. Telephone inventor Alexander Graham Bell started the event around 4:00 PM Eastern Standard Time by speaking from New York to his assistant Thomas A. Watson in San Francisco. Mr. Vail and others including William Rockefeller and J. P. Morgan Jr. listened to the conversation keenly in one of the parlors of the Jekyll Island clubhouse.

SEAFOOD SALAD IN ARTICHOKES

1/3	cup vegetable oil		1/2	cup each: diced radishes and chopped onion
2	tablespoons vinegar		1/4	cup finely chopped parsley
1/2	teaspoon salt		6	large California artichokes, cooked and chilled
1/8	teaspoon pepper			
1	pound cooked shrimp, crab meat, lobster, or combination		2	medium tomatoes cut into sixths
4	hard-cooked eggs, coarsely chopped			parsley sprigs
1	cup diced celery			Lemon Mayonnaise

Assemble ingredients and utensils. Blend oil, vinegar, salt, and pepper in large bowl. Add seafood, eggs, celery, radishes, onion, and parsley; toss gently. Cover and chill several hours. At serving time, prepare artichokes for stuffing by gently pushing leaves outward; remove fuzzy centers. Fill artichokes with seafood salad garnish each with tomato wedges and a parsley sprig. Serve with Lemon mayonnaise.

Yields 6 main-dish servings

LEMON MAYONNAISE

Blend 2/3 cup mayonnaise, 1 teaspoon lemon juice, and 1 to 2 teaspoons prepared mustard in small bowl. Turn into small serving dish and garnish with a slice of lemon. Use as dressing for salad and as dip for artichoke leaves.

Yields 2/3 cup

MANDARIN SALAD WITH POPPY SEED DRESSING

2	tablespoons wine vinegar
1	teaspoon Dijon mustard
1/2	teaspoon salt
1/8	teaspoon cayenne pepper
1	tablespoon honey
6	tablespoons vegetable oil
1 1/2	teaspoons poppy seed
1	small head of lettuce, rinsed, drained, and chilled
1	small red onion
1	11-ounce can mandarin oranges, drained

Assemble ingredients and utensils. Combine first 7 ingredients and shake well. Tear lettuce into bite-sized pieces. Peel and slice onion into very thin rings. Combine lettuce, onion, and oranges. Toss with dressing in large salad bowl.

Yields 4 to 6 servings

PUMPKIN BREAD

1	cup water
1	cup vegetable oil
1	can pumpkin pie filling or 1 can plain pumpkin
3	cups sugar
3	eggs
1	cup chopped black walnuts
1 1/2	cups chopped dates
3 1/2	cups self-rising flour
1	teaspoon each: nutmeg, ginger, and salt
1/2	teaspoon cloves
1/2	teaspoon baking powder
2	teaspoons cinnamon
2	teaspoons baking soda

Assemble ingredients and utensils. Mix first 7 ingredients in large mixing bowl. Sift together remaining ingredients. Combine with pumpkin mixture. Pour into 2 large greased 9x5-inch loaf pans. Bake in a 325-degree oven for 1 1/2 hours.

Yields 2 loaves

FANTASTIC FUDGE

2/3 cup evaporated milk
2/3 cup butter or margarine
3 cups sugar
1 12-ounce package Hershey's semi-sweet chocolate chips

1 7-ounce jar marshmallow crème
1 cup coarsely chopped nuts
1 teaspoon vanilla

Assemble ingredients and utensils. Combine evaporated milk, butter, and sugar in a heavy 2 1/2 to 3-quart saucepan. Bring to full rolling boil, stirring constantly to prevent scorching. Boil 5 minutes over medium heat or until candy thermometer reaches 234 degrees, continue to stir constantly. Remove from heat; stir in chocolate chips until melted. Add marshmallow crème, nuts, and vanilla; beat until well blended. Pour into greased 8- or 9-inch square pan. Cool; cut into squares.

Yields about 3 pounds of fudge

ZUCCHINI BREAD

3	eggs	1/4	teaspoon baking powder
1	cup vegetable oil	2	teaspoons baking soda
1 1/2	cups sugar	3	teaspoons ground cinnamon
2	cups zucchini, grated, well-drained	1	teaspoon salt
2	teaspoons vanilla	1	cup raisins
2	cups all-purpose flour, sifted	1	cup walnuts or pecans, chopped

Assemble ingredients and utensils. Beat eggs lightly in large bowl. Stir in oil, sugar, zucchini, and vanilla. Sift flour, baking powder, soda, cinnamon, and salt onto waxed paper. Stir into egg mixture until well-blended; stir in raisins and nuts. Spoon batter into two well-greased 8x5x3-inch loaf pans. Bake in a 375-degree oven for 1 hour or until the center springs back when lightly pressed with finger. Cool on wire rack 10 minutes. Remove from pans and cool completely.

Yields 2 loaves

Variation: Omit raisins and add one-half teaspoon grated lemon peel.

JEKYLL ISLAND CREAMY SHRIMP BISQUE

1	small onion, chopped
2	stalks celery, chopped
1	small carrot, chopped salad oil, as needed
1/2	cup Arborio rice, raw
1/2	cup white wine
3	quarts shrimp stock
2–3	pounds, shrimp peeled and deveined
	salt and white pepper, to taste

1	tablespoon paprika
2	teaspoons chili powder
1	teaspoon cumin
2	tablespoons fresh parsley, washed, chopped
2	teaspoons dry dill
1	quart heavy cream
1/2	cup sherry

Assemble ingredients and utensils. Sauté vegetables in oil until translucent; add rice and sauté two more minutes. Deglaze with white wine and reduce by half, stirring often. Add stock, shrimp, herbs, and spices. Cook for about 45 minutes, until rice is fully cooked and coming apart. Puree completely with food processor. Add cream and bring back to simmer. Adjust seasonings and then add the sherry. Remove from heat and cool down.

Yields 1 gallon

Courtesy of the Jekyll Island Club's Chef's collection.

JEKYLL POT PIE

1	pound 51/70 shrimp, peeled and deveined	4 1/2	cups water
1	pound bay scallops	1 1/2	cups heavy cream
1	small red bell pepper, diced	2	ounces whiskey
1	small green bell pepper, diced	1	tablespoon dry dill weed
1	pint button mushrooms, quartered		salt and pepper to taste
			slurry (cornstarch and water mixed) to taste

Assemble ingredients and utensils. Poach veggies in water, take out and poach seafood for 3 minutes, add the veggies back. Add cream and dill, bring to a simmer. Season with salt and pepper, add slurry and simmer 1 more minute. Take off heat and add whiskey. Serve in a bouclé shell or baked puff pastry shell.

Yields 8 servings

Courtesy of the Jekyll Island Club's Chef's collection.

CANDIED SWEET POTATOES

6	medium sweet potatoes	1	tablespoon melted butter
1	cup orange juice	1/3	cup packed brown sugar
2	teaspoons grated orange rind	1/3	cup sugar
1	teaspoon cornstarch		salt to taste

Assemble ingredients and utensils. In a saucepan, combine sweet potatoes with enough water to cover. Cook until tender, but firm. Cool. Remove skins. Leave sweet potatoes whole or cut lengthwise into 1/2 inch slices. Arrange in baking dish. Combine orange juice, orange rind, and cornstarch in saucepan; mix well. Add melted butter, brown sugar, sugar, and salt. Cook on medium heat until thickened, stirring constantly. Spoon evenly over sweet potatoes. Bake, covered, at 350 degrees for 20 minutes; remove cover. Bake for 15 minutes longer or until heated to serving temperature.

Yields 6 servings

BREAD PUDDING WITH BRANDY SAUCE

10	slices day-old bread, crusts removed		1	teaspoon ground cinnamon
4	cups whole milk, scalded		1/2	teaspoon ground nutmeg
1	cup heavy cream		1/4	cup butter, melted
4	eggs		1/2	cup seedless raisins
1	cup sugar			whipped cream for garnish
1	teaspoon vanilla			

Assemble ingredients and utensils. In a large bowl, break bread into pieces and combine with milk and heavy cream. In another bowl, beat eggs; add sugar and the next 5 ingredients. Pour over bread mixture. Pour into a 3-quart baking dish; place dish into pan of warm water. Bake in a preheated 350-degree oven for 1 1/2 hours. Serve brandy sauce over warm pudding and top with whipped cream.

Yields 8 servings

BRANDY SAUCE

3	egg yolks		1	tablespoon cornstarch
1	cup sugar		1/4	cup water
1	teaspoon vanilla		1 1/2	ounces brandy
1 1/2	cups whole milk			

In a saucepan, lightly beat yolks; add sugar, vanilla, and milk; heat. Blend cornstarch into water; stir into hot mixture. Continue cooking until thickened. Remove from heat and stir in brandy. Cool and serve over pudding.

COLD TOMATO SOUP

12	large fresh tomatoes, peeled and seeded
3	medium onions, chopped
1/3	cup chopped celery
2	teaspoons salt
1	teaspoon pepper
1	teaspoon sugar
1/2	teaspoon dried basil
6	tablespoons butter
1	pint sour cream
	fresh basil or dill for garnish

Assemble ingredients and utensils. Sauté tomatoes, onion, celery, salt, pepper, sugar, and dried basil in butter until soft, about 30 minutes. Pour into blender or food processor and puree. Chill before serving. When ready to serve stir in sour cream. Garnish with fresh basil or dill.

Yields 10 to 12 servings

FRONT PORCH LEMONADE

1 1/4	cups sugar
1/2	cup boiling water
1 1/2	cups fresh lemon juice
4 1/2	cups cold water
10	lemon slices

Assemble all ingredients and utensils. In a saucepan, bring water to boiling. In a heat-proof pitcher, combine sugar and boiling water. Stir until sugar dissolves. Add lemon juice and cold water. Stir well. Chill until serving time. Pour into ice filled glasses. Garnish with lemon slices.

Yields 10 servings

BEAUTIFUL TREASURES
IN FAITH CHAPEL

The incredibly wealthy members of the club spared no expense or creativity when building their place of worship on the island. Built in 1904, Faith Chapel is reminiscent of an early Colonial meetinghouse, but it also incorporates Gothic style decorative elements such as exterior terra cotta gargoyles and six carved heads, called grotesques, which adorn the interior trusses. The small building with its richly stained cypress wood interior houses an unexpected masterpiece by one of America's most famous artists. Glimmering in the sunlight is the magnificent stained glass designed, installed, and signed by Louis Tiffany himself. It was not, however, original to the 1904 construction, but was commissioned as a dedicatory window entitled David Sets Singers Unto the Lord, for Frederick Bourne, the club's fourth president, and installed in 1921. On the other side of the chapel above the alter is a second superb example of American stained glass—Adoration of the Christ Child—designed and fabricated by David Maitland Armstrong, one of Tiffany's students, and his daughter Helen. Made of several layers of glass, giving the illusion of depth, it is one of the most outstanding pieces of stained glass in the nation.

CRANBERRY CHUTNEY

4	cups fresh cranberries	1/4	teaspoon salt
1	apple, peeled and diced	1/4	cloves, ginger
1/2	cup seedless raisins	1/2	teaspoon allspice
1/2	cup golden raisins	1	tablespoon Dijon mustard
2	cups light brown sugar	1	whole cinnamon stick
3/4	cup apple cider vinegar		

Assemble ingredients and utensils. Combine all ingredients in a large saucepan; bring to a boil, stirring occasionally. Reduce heat and simmer uncovered about 30 minutes. Stir often. Cool. Refrigerate.

Yields 1 1/2 pints

NEW GOLF COURSE

JEKYLL ISLAND ALMOND GROUPER

2   6-ounce pieces fresh grouper
1   tbsp + 1 tbsp olive oil
    salt and pepper to taste, sprinkle on both
    sides of grouper
1/2 teaspoon fresh garlic, minced
1/2 teaspoon herbs de Province or fresh
    chopped parsley

3   tablespoons almond slivers, toasted
2   teaspoons lemon juice
1/4 cup white wine
3   ounces whole butter
    salt and pepper to taste

Assemble ingredients and utensils. Preheat oven to 350 degrees. Heat sauté pan over medium heat, add 1 tablespoon olive oil. Season the grouper with the salt and pepper and place both filets in the pan. Sear on both sides for 1 to 2 minutes. Remove the fish from the pan and transfer to an ovenproof baking dish. Put the fish in the oven for about 5 minutes or until it is cooked. Meanwhile, add the other 1 tbsp of oil to the fish pan. Add the garlic and herbs and sauté over medium for about 1 minute. Add the almonds, wine, and lemon juice and let reduce by half. Turn heat off and add the butter to the almond sauce 1 ounce at a time. Stir sauce to melt butter. Sprinkle with salt and pepper to taste. Spoon sauce over grouper and enjoy!

Yields 2 servings

Courtesy of the Jekyll Island Club's Chef's collection.

JEKYLL ISLAND FARMERS' POT

1	carrot, peeled, diced	16–24	ounces tomato juice, depending on how juicy you want it.
3	stalks celery, diced		
1	small onion, diced		
1	zucchini, diced	1	tablespoon garlic, minced
2	squash, diced	2	teaspoons basil, chopped
3	broccoli florets, diced	2	teaspoons thyme, chopped
1/4	head cauliflower, chopped into bite size pieces	2	tablespoons parsley, minced
2	cans diced tomatoes	2	teaspoons fresh rosemary, chopped
6	ounces tomato puree		salt and pepper, to taste

Assemble ingredients and utensils. In a large pot, sauté carrots, celery, and onions. Add fresh vegetables, garlic, and herbs. Sauté and add all of the tomatoes and juice. Simmer for 30 minutes; adjust seasonings with salt and pepper.

Yields 4 to 6 servings

Courtesy of the Jekyll Island Club's Chef's collection.

SHRIMP MOLD

1   10 3/4 ounce can tomato
    soup
1   8-ounce package cream
    cheese, softened and cut
    into chunks
3   envelopes plain gelatin,
    softened for 5 minutes
6   tablespoons water
2   pounds cooked small shrimp

1/4   cup diced green onion
1/4   cup diced green pepper
1/4   teaspoon each: salt, pepper,
      celery salt, onion salt, and
      hot sauce
1   cup mayonnaise
2   tablespoons horseradish,
      drained

Assemble ingredients and utensils. Heat soup and cream cheese. Stir with wire whisk until cheese is melted. Some small lumps will remain. Dissolve gelatin in 6 table-spoons water; add to hot soup mixture. Remove from heat and stir well. Add remaining ingredients. Pour into a well-greased 1-quart ring mold. Refrigerate until firm. Garnish as desired.

Yields 40 to 50 servings as an appetizer spread

SOUR CREAM CHOCOLATE CAKE

2	cups all-purpose flour
2	cups sugar
1	cup water
3/4	cup sour cream
1/4	cup butter
1 1/4	teaspoons baking soda
1	teaspoon salt

1	teaspoon vanilla
1/2	teaspoon baking powder
2	eggs
4	1-ounce squares unsweetened baking chocolate, melted

Assemble ingredients and utensils. Measure all of the ingredients for the cake into a large bowl of mixer and beat for 30 seconds at low speed, scraping sides of bowl constantly; then beat for 3 minutes at high speed. Pour into greased and floured cake pans, either 2 9-inch pans or 3 8-inch pans. Bake in a preheated 350-degree oven for 20 to 25 minutes. Remove from the oven and cool on racks. Frost.

Yields 8 to 10 servings

FROSTING

1/2	cup butter
4	1-ounce squares unsweetened baking chocolate

4	cups confectioners' sugar
1	cup sour cream
2	teaspoons vanilla

In the top of a double boiler, melt butter and chocolate over barely simmering water. Remove from heat and cool. Add confectioners' sugar, blend in sour cream and vanilla, and beat until smooth. Put frosting between each of the layers of the cake, on the top, and all around the sides.

CHERRY COLA SALAD

3/4	cup water
3/4	cup sugar
1	16-ounce can cherry pie filling
1	large package cherry gelatin
1	teaspoon lemon juice
1	med. can crushed pineapple
1	cup chopped pecans
1	16-ounce cola

Assemble ingredients and utensils. Mix water and sugar in medium sauce pan and bring to boil. Add cherry pie filling, bring to boil, remove from heat, and stir in gelatin. Add lemon juice, pineapple, nuts, and cola; stir well. Pour into covered container and refrigerate.

Yields 6 servings

THE BIRTH OF THE FEDERAL RESERVE

History was made on Jekyll Island in 1910 when the framework for the Federal Reserve Act was drafted in the clubhouse. In October of 1907, several banking firms collapsed as depositors withdrew funds for fear of unwise investments and misuse of money. Several banking leaders including Jekyll Island Club members George F. Baker, president of the First National Bank, and James Stillman, president of National City Bank, met with financier J. Pierpont Morgan and began examining the assets of the troubled institutions. In November of 1910 Senator Aldrich invited several bankers, economic scholars, and many of the country's leading financiers, who together represented about one-fourth of the world's wealth, to attend a conference on Jekyll Island to discuss monetary policy and the banking system. While meeting under the ruse of a duck-shooting excursion, the financial experts were in reality hunting for a way to restructure America's banking system and eliminate the possibility of future economic panics. The conference's solution to America's banking problems called for the creation of a central bank. Although congress did not pass the reform bill submitted by Senator Aldrich, it did approve a similar proposal in 1913 called the Federal Reserve Act. The Federal Reserve System of today mirrors in essence the plan developed on Jekyll Island in 1910.

JACK DANIEL'S MINT JULEP FOR TWENTY

1	cup sugar
6	ounces ice water
30	or more tender mint leaves, divided
36	ounces Jack Daniel's Tennessee Sippin' Whiskey
	crushed ice
	small punch bowl or 1/2 gallon pitcher

Assemble ingredients and utensils. Pour sugar and water combination in bottom of punch bowl or pitcher. Add 10 mint leaves. Carefully bruise the leaves but do not crush them because this releases the bitter, inner juices. Pack the punch bowl or pitcher with crushed ice and pour whiskey to cover. Stir with a long spoon and move contents up and down for a few minutes. Add more whiskey if necessary. Pour mixture into individual silver julep cups or hi-ball glasses and refrigerate for 10 minutes to frost the glass. When ready to serve, garnish with 20 additional mint leaves.

Courtesy of the Jekyll Island Club's Chef's collection.

JEKYLL ISLAND CLUB SHRIMP-N-GRITS

1   pound fresh Georgia white shrimp,
     peeled and deveined
1   bundle green onion, diced
1/2 pound Andouille sausage (or any other
     spicy sausage you prefer)

flour as needed
white wine to taste
1/2 squeezed lemon
1   cup heavy whipping cream
Old Bay seasoning to taste

GARLIC BUTTER FOR SAUTÉ

Soften 1 pound unsalted butter, 6 ounces bacon fat, 2 tablespoons minced garlic, 1 tablespoon paprika, 1/2 teaspoon each chopped thyme, parsley, oregano. Mix all ingredients together and set aside for later use.

CHEESE GRITS

Follow recipe on package except use chicken stock instead of water. The grits should be stiff. Add medium sharp cheddar cheese to taste; add salt and pepper to taste. Set aside but keep warm. In sauté pan, add garlic butter. Add sausage and onions let sauté, then add shrimp, cream, wine, and lemon let cook for 3 minutes. Add Old Bay, salt and pepper to taste. Let simmer, then sprinkle flour on top and mix in. Continue until right consistency. Simmer a little while longer to cook out flour taste, and then serve. Use some of the leftover butter on French bread; grill and serve with the shrimp and grits. Put grits in bowl and top with shrimp mixture, ready to eat.

Yields 6 to 8 servings

Courtesy of the Jekyll Island Club's Chef's collection.

PORK LOIN ROAST WITH HERBS

3	pounds pork loin, bone in or out	2	teaspoons kosher or sea salt
1/4	cup sage, chopped	1	teaspoon black pepper, coarse ground
1/4	cup marjoram or oregano, chopped	1	teaspoon nutmeg, ground
2	tablespoons garlic, chopped	3	teaspoons olive oil
2	tablespoons dry mustard	2	cups chicken stock
1/4	cup Dijon mustard	2	tablespoons unsalted butter

Assemble ingredients and utensils. In a blender place herbs, garlic, mustard, salt, pepper, and nutmeg and puree with olive oil. Set aside. Butterfly pork loin to 1/2-inch thickness. Evenly spread herb paste across pork and roll up like a cigar. Tie with butchers or roasting twine, place in roasting pan with chicken stock. Cover with foil and bake at 250 degrees for about 1/2 hour. Remove foil, finish baking at 375 degrees another 15 minutes. Remove from oven, and allow to rest for 10 minutes on cutting board. Slice and serve with pan sauce. Place liquid left in pan into saucepan. Reduce to 1/4 cup over medium heat. Remove from heat, whisk in the butter. Adjust seasoning as necessary and serve with pork loin.

CAVIAR POTATOES

2–3	pounds bite-sized new potatoes	1/4	cup mayonnaise
1	pint sour cream	2	teaspoons lemon juice
1	2-ounce jar caviar chives, chopped	2	tablespoons grated onion
1	3-ounce package cream cheese	1	teaspoon Worcestershire sauce

Assemble ingredients and utensils. Boil potatoes in salted water approximately 20 minutes or until tender. Drain and cool. Using a melon ball scoop, hollow out the top of the potato. Fill cavity with sour cream. Top filling with caviar and sprinkle with chives. As a variation, mix remaining ingredients and fill cavity with mixture.

Yields filling for 2 to 3 pounds new potatoes

COCKTAIL OYSTERS

1/2 cup finely chopped onion	1 teaspoon garlic salt
2 tablespoons butter	1/4 teaspoon hot sauce
1 cup catsup	1 pint oysters, well drained
2 tablespoons Worcestershire sauce	

Assemble ingredients and utensils. Sauté onion in butter. Add catsup, Worcestershire sauce, garlic salt, and hot sauce; heat to boiling. Add oysters; heat only until edges of oysters curl. Serve hot in chafing dish with Melba toast rounds.

Yields 3 cups

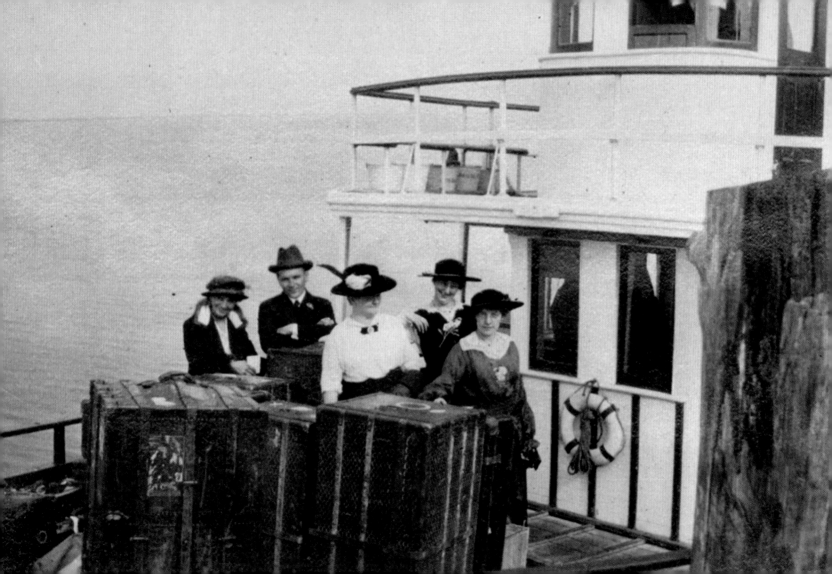

SHERRIED VIDALIAS

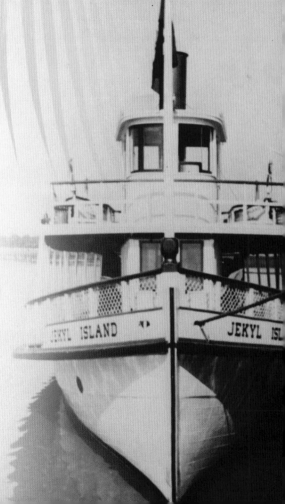

5	medium Vidalia onions, sliced	1/2	teaspoon black pepper
1/3	cup unsalted butter, melted	1/2	cup dry sherry
1	teaspoon sugar	2	dashes hot sauce
1/2	teaspoon salt	2	tablespoons grated Parmesan cheese

Assemble all ingredients and utensils. Sauté onion slices in butter in a Dutch oven over medium heat for 5 to 8 minutes or until crisp-tender. Sprinkle with sugar, salt, and pepper; stir gently to separate into rings. Add sherry and hot sauce; simmer 2 to 3 minutes. Sprinkle with cheese and serve immediately.

Yields 6 to 8 servings

COLD LIME SOUFFLÉ

1	envelope unflavored gelatin		1	tablespoon lime zest, grated
1/4	cup cold water		6	egg whites
4	egg yolks		1/2	cup sugar
1/2	cup lime juice		1	cup heavy cream, whipped
1/2	cup sugar			sweetened flaked coconut,
1/2	teaspoon salt			lightly toasted for garnish

Assemble ingredients and utensils. In a small bowl, sprinkle gelatin over water to soften. In the top of a double boiler, mix egg yolks, lime juice, sugar, and salt. Cook mixture over simmering water until slightly thickened; remove from heat. Stir in softened gelatin and lime zest; stir mixture until gelatin is completely dissolved. Cool. In a small bowl, beat egg whites until stiff; gradually beat in sugar until whites hold peaks. Fold whipped heavy cream and egg whites into lime mixture. Spoon into soufflé dish. Chill. Sprinkle with coconut flakes before serving.

Yields 4 to 6 servings

For More Information, Reservations, and Event Planning

The Jekyll Island Authority

1.877.4.JEKYLL

100 James Road Jekyll Island, GA 31527

www.jekyllisland.com

&

Jekyll Island Club Hotel

800.535.9547

371 Riverview Drive Jekyll Island, GA 31527

www.jekyllclub.com

DESCRIPTION OF PHOTOGRAPHS

Unless otherwise noted, photographic images are provided courtesy of the Jekyll Island Museum—a division of the Jekyll Island Authority.
The many images contributed by Mary Lawson Photography are identified as MLP at the end of each description.
Special thanks to Harlan Hambright for the use of his images indicated by HH.

RECIPE INDEX